THE
NORFOLK
POEMS
OF
HAYDEN
CARRUTH

[1 JUNE TO 1 SEPTEMBER 1961]

This time was a lovingkindness, J and Ann,
A summer, unrepayable. All a man
May keep are the leaves flung off as our green wave ran.
Dry leaves, can they be thanks? Perhaps they can.

THE PRAIRIE PRESS
IOWA CITY

CONTENTS

A Short-Run View

"In the long run aesthetics is the study of the unattain-
able, if not the unknowable. . . ."–Marcus of Pavonia.

I AM speaking here of beauty in all its aspects.
The town of Norfolk is situate, as lawyers say,
Interjacent to Canaan and Winsted on Rt. 44
In the high valley of the Blackberry River, tightly
Bedded in the Litchfield Hills—a lateral appendage
Of the lower Berkshires; Massachusetts lies
Four miles north. If it possessed no other
Distinction, Norfolk would be the world's creditor
Each June for its rhododendron and mountain laurel.
In fact, however, it enjoys other marks of favor.
Although the town cherishes its genteel repose,
It contains, for instance, three notable oddballs,
Brendan Gill, James Laughlin, and the undersigned.
On Bald Mountain View Road lives a cow that tilts,
Not against windmills, but against small open
Sports cars—a most Lawrentian cow. The post office
In Norfolk is the ugliest post office ever built
In the United States or dominions, but it houses
By far the best postal staff. There are a number
Of millionaires in Norfolk, which adds a good deal
To the scenery, but also a number of people who are
Content not to be millionaires, which adds even more.
Norfolk is cold in the winter; it is called
"The Ice-Box of Connecticut," and the local agent
Of the federal weather bureau has been enjoined

[9]

By the real estate interests to place his thermometer
In Ted Childs's swamp, the warmest part of town,
So as not to frighten away the prospective buyers.
One year there was frost in every month, so
I am told by Mrs. Barnes, whose family has lived
In Norfolk for generations; like other proper
Norfolkians, she pronounces it Norfork. I
Recommend to the Ritz the strawberries of
A. M. Eaton and the sweet corn sold under the sign
Of Native Fresh Vegetables on the road to Canaan.
The Smyth's retriever is named Chet, after Chet
Huntley. Mr. Hayes, proprietor of the Esso Station
On the Winsted Road, specializes in the upkeep
Of classical cars, e.g. 1925 Lincolns and 1937
Cords, but his work on all cars is of a high order.
The village green contains the most magnificently
Priapic fountain I have ever seen in America,
And also, painted on a board and tacked to an elm,
The worst poem on the subject of trees I have ever
Read; considering Kilmer, it is a feat of
Remarkable ingenuity. The library, on the other
Hand, possesses a good selection of books
And a reading room where smoking is permitted.
Astonishing! There are many foreign cars, but
Only two properly classifiable as sports cars,
My dilapidated MG and a gleaming red Triumph
That lives by the Canaan Road. In summer
The Yale School of Music and Art produces,
In addition to a certain amount of moonstaring

And handholding on the village green, music,
Excellent music, and art, not so excellent;
And on Canaan Mountain the Yale Arboretum for
The Study of Tree Genetics also produces music,
A slower and possibly even more excellent harmony.
But Ted Childs knows more about trees than anyone.
Here is a catalogue of some local placenames:
Tobey Pond, Tibbals Hill, Haystack Mountain,
Turkey Cobble, Crissey Pond, Wangum Pond, Great
Bear Swamp, Old Man McMullen Pond, Lovers Lane
(A paved street, with no apostrophe), the redundant
Pond Hill Pond, the Mad River (which washed away
A good bit of Winsted five years ago), College Hill
(Not an academy in sight), and just over the line
In Massachusetts, East Indies Pond—I don't know
Why. My favorite is Seldom Seen Pond, unknown
Except to the U.S. geological surveyors. We have
A fantastic organization called the Norfolk
Curling Club; I have not seen it in action,
But I hope they use highland whisky. Also:
Ye Olde Newgate Coon Club, the Doolittle Club,
The Country Club, and in fact more clubs than a
Self-respecting town of 2000 souls ought to allow;
To say nothing of the Norfolk Savings Bank, which is
A cavern of gloom and I suspect also the last strong-
Hold of the Lower Berkshire Anti-Jeffersonian Society.
A few other names must be included: the Hauges
And the beautiful Rose Marie, Mrs. Tyrrell,
Leon & Dorothy Deloy, Mahalia Fields, Theodore

Sylvernale (a dead shot), Wonza Hunt, the Drs.
Barstow and Blatz, Izzy Tadiello, and Joe
Pallone.* The famous residents of Norfolk—five or
Six in number—will get no additional publicity here.
I myself live in the woods near Tobey Pond; I am
A newcomer, but if Norfolkians disdain my views
As mere first impressions, let them think twice,
Lest a longer acquaintanceship should prove me wrong
Not only as a critic but as a panegyrist.

*Addenda on proof: Nor may I neglect Leila (the
Lovely), my friend Paul, Tanio, Annie Dixon,
The younglings (Robert, Henry, Leon, and Bry),
Mrs. Bellamy, Miss O'Connell, and of course
Joanie Curtiss—but many shall go unnamed.

Tibbals Hill

"Das Ewig-Weibliche zieht uns hinan."

"Meghaloke bhavati sukhinopyanyatha chittavrittih
  Kanthaslesha pranayini jane kim punar durasamsthe."

CHARMED elephant, tickled pink cloud, my traipser
Sauntering on hilltops like a young latecomer,
Shall I shout hurry, hurry in the eye-blue field
We call in our deep midsummer
The Field of Heaven? Shall I? Can the miles be healed?

Messenger, why do you gambol, why do you idle,
Turning aside for so much as a pretty nothing,
A lake in the fernland, birches on top of a hill?
O cloud, you are a slow thing
To take a soft word out where the sea-winds shrill!

Haven't you already seen the wide world, loiterer?
Selfish! The hell with a little cloud's delighting,
Strayed like any fool lordling gone in the woods
Or maybe fishing or kiting
While the work waits and we scour the neighborhoods.

Yes, I am sore-minded. And I cannot trust you.
The Atlantic waves, see how they toss and mingle,
See how they serry longly like the desert sands;
And tonight I'll lie down single;
And tonight she'll rove in God knows what far lands.

You, my fuzzyhead, could you remember a message
Even if somehow you should surmount the ocean?
My word would leak like spume from your dewy brain.
And besides, in all the commotion
How will you find her or know her? Loafer, explain!

I must describe her? Ah, but the words are threadbare.
The swarming wordeaters, pests!—they've sucked the juices.
Then, cloud, be content. Know that she has such arms
As only the sea adduces
From deodar smoothly and cleanly, and the sun then warms.

Know that her hands discourse more delicately
Than this poor wisp which you so archly brandish,
And that like gentian the lash lies on her eye,
And moreover that all outlandish
Fashion befits her, though I cannot tell you why.

I ask you, cloud, in your journeying over grainland
Have you not seen the wheat many-hued, soft-blowing
In intrinsic dance? On such land, little cloud,
I have once done my sowing,
Belly and thigh, gold-blonde and earthen-proud.

Proud, schmoud—it is useless! Hear then two sorrows.
First, the long nights that keep for sleeping. Second
(And this, my bundle of fog, bears all the fate),
A loveliness has beckoned
And I am red hot to go, but I must wait.

Because, because . . . always I live in making,
The making lives in hurt, the hurt in distance.
Coming together kills hurt and kills the life.
Damn, damn, goddamn such persistence,
The imagination eating the blade of a knife.

The worst (or not the worst—who's your master?)
Is this: the made thing at once goes soaring,
Up, up, a cloud, a bloody cloud, so thin,
So far from any imploring,
That there is, once it is made, no discipline

Can ever keep it, but it must go beyond me,
Tricking and ambling idly, disappearing
Over the hills, breaking in wide-fallen notes,
Leaving me out of hearing,
The same old hatful of idiot anecdotes.

Maybe tomorrow will be time enough for soaring.
Poet, run, run at last, the sun on your shoulder,
Wind tugging the hair-roots. Come, if you must have love,
Old Peg o' the Loft is older
By two days since Tuesday but still meets a thrust with
        a shove.

In Tobey Woods

AT NOONTIME under the very tall pines
Heat is a half-light and nothing moves
Unless it is one deathly shell-white moth
Fluttering, fluttering.

And the woods are very quiet, unless
It is one vireo idiotically tzekking,
Tzekking.

Stillness; the deep stillness.

I wish my mind would not revert
To that time I was a bedlamite
At chess with the blushing Irish nurse
While the coprolaliac young lawyer
Cursed his father the judge in words
I would not whisper into a pit.

Maureen, Maureen, why did I not go
To seek you in the clean fields of Ireland?

Bhava

IF I AM very lucky someday I think
I'll take a mistress from Bhubaneswar,
But let her be classical of the type, I ask;
Atibhanga, meaning extreme flexion,
The mesial dropped from her left pupil through
The heart, thence rightward of the navel. Let
Her illustrate the manual: the torso ("her
Most perfect part") made like a tender creeper,
Her fingers like the champaka in full bloom,
Her palm the wide-cupped lotus, and her eyes
Two petals therefrom, and her nose the flower
They call the til. Tritely, her neck should be
The swan's, her waist the delicate lioness's.
Thighs, ascending, move like the plantain trunk.
Her only garment is her skirt, well weighted
With jewels along the hem to make it fall
More gracefully, but otherwise transparent;
And she must carry "flowing ornaments"
Around her neck and "poised between the breasts."
Maybe she will take heed to come to me
With four arms. I hope so. What embraces,
What caresses! It's almost more than. . . . Sweetheart,
Do make haste, while my luck is running strong.

The Wild Swans at Norfolk

To BEGIN with there are
No wild swans at Norfolk,
This other Norfolk
Where James Laughlin lives
With his red-haired Ann.

There are towhees and wrens
And soft yellow sapsuckers
And Blackburnian warblers
And gray owls and barred owls
And flickers but there are
No wild swans.

I can invent the swans.
They wheel on thunder's
Hundred throbbing wings
Down the sweet curve
Of Tobey Pond, pounding
The blocks of air
As trains in my childhood
Pounded their rails.

They are real wild swans;
And even though this summer
I turn forty and am deserted
By the young woman I love,
I have grown sick of emblems.

I have seen this place
On the map, and the names of
The people of Norfolk appear
On voting lists and tax rolls.

Hear how the swans converse
(As they break wing for landing)
In a rude, lightning tongue.
I cannot understand,
But clearly the swans know
What they are talking about.

Meadow House

THIS is a poem for you, Ann. Impromptu,
Falling out of my precipitate brain faster
Than light dropping through a torn cloud.

And the typewriter lags. Catch up, I say!
How the wood and stone must have lagged for
Wright looking at a trance-house on a hill.

At least you and I have the advantage of not
Being architects, who fret in houses they build
And go thoroughly mad in houses they do not build.

You can live in a house. Wright wouldn't have liked
Meadow House, his style being something different,
But Meadow House lives on the hill naturally.

As naturally as the birches. And Mr. Wright
With his artist's complacency could not believe
That houses grow and very seldom are built.

(Poems too. As the light grows when it plunges
Through the torn cloud like a taproot seeking
The needed humane sustenance for heaven.)

The house grew on the hill, the woman grew
In the house, the birches grew in the meadow,
The hill is growing, I see it change every day.

No one knows why. Growing is a word
That has never been defined, not even in
My huge thirty-five-dollar dictionary.

But the end of growth, which never really ends,
Is always perfection, even if ugly or sore,
Because growth proceeds by means of balances.

(And the end of growth is always a phase
To be left behind. And real ugliness
Does not grow but arises from destruction.)

Of course Meadow House has nothing ugly;
Only balances, arrangements in which I move
Without seeming to make any displacement.

I hope there is none, because this is what
I knew many years ago and then forgot,
Forgot. It is the service of friendliness.

Ho-Hum Again

HAVING lost the woman I loved
    I am of course heartbroken,
In a dying summer embarked on war
When many good folk are heartsore
    And one heart is a small token.

Too small to be taken seriously.
    Death creeps in the air like pollen,
Seeding amazement in lovely eyes,
Hers too that were my enterprise
    When reason had not fallen.

Comparative Iconography

GIVE it what name you choose,
In all lands the female symbol is a hole,
And where I come from the people use
The eye-socket of a skull.

Purana, Meaning Once Upon a Time

ONLY the gods may act with perfect impudence—
That is, irrationally. Listen while I retell
A story from a book as old as the Tobey Woods.

It fell on an autumn night, when the forest leaves
Moved like small rustling animals over the moss
And Jumna flowed with a sure deep-running strength,

That Sri Krishna played his flute by the riverbank
And the moonlight dripped like rain from tangled trees.
The music of love came liquidly to the village

Where gopis, who were the milkmaids, drank willlessly,
Their souls tipped to the song in unimagined thirst;
And soon they ran unresistingly to the forest,

One by one, and in groups, tripping and hurrying,
Leaving parents, brothers, sisters, husbands behind,
Leaving their babies whimpering in the cradles.

They said: "Ah, heavily love-laden we will give all."
Conceive the bewilderment in their eyes when Krishna,
Surrounded, the good looks of him bruising the girls,

Rebuked them, saying: "What! Have you come in the night?
Through the forest? Then you care nothing for tigers?
Shame! Respectable girls running after a lover

In the night, sacrificing your lords and your parents,
Your brothers and sisters and children. Pretty girls,
Go back to your places, go back and be content."

Tears melted their eyes and their hearts were frightened;
They looked miserably at one another in their confusion,
And began to scratch the ground with their feet like deer.

At last they said: "Truly we must attend our husbands
And our parents and children, but O Sweet Lord,
When thou art husband, parent, and child is it not just

That we seek the pleasures of all of these in Thee?"
The All-One turned away and I think said nothing,
And sorely, wearily the milkmaids returned to the village,

Their question unanswered. The singing hermit thrush
In Tobey Woods has brought this to my mind.
The leaves are beginning to fall. Soon he will be gone.

Improvisation on a Theme by Mrs. Pomeroy

NOTICE this strange mystique
Condemning self-pity:
We call a man weak
Or even dotty

Whom we may hear bemoaning
His long nightwatch,
And girls seem unbecoming
Who cry too much.

Christ, aren't we all such creatures
As in the soul
And flesh of our born natures
Are pitiful?

Consider the human death.
No full stop
Comes when the stifling breath
Merely gives up,

But for a certain moment
Warmth remains,
The packed cells stay animate
While the spirit drains.

In a deathly, draining world,
Though very nervous,
Thus we stay, keeping curled
To someone who'll love us.

Well, I have been forsaken,
Like some of you;
My friends, you are not mistaken,
I am pitiful too.

On Canaan Mountain Meadow

OF COURSE, mankind—and the brain of it, brawn of it;
Enormous, as I too have marveled many a time
And will again.

But today its littleness I would moderately disparage,
That makes the stone a thing that is less than stone,
A dolmen, a god.

I say the stone is a greatness, itself in its grain,
Meaning more than a meaning, and more than a mind
May diminish.

In the sun in the field in the churchly changes of weather,
The stone lies ample and smooth and warm and brown
And at the same time blonde.

I am stroking the stone with my fingers and my curved palm,
And it is as soft as linen, and flows like the flax
From the spindle.

I would lie on the stone, reaching my arms down strongly
To draw myself full to the stone and to fondle
The flesh-gloss below.

I would copulate with the stone until I became like stone,
A slow, long spasm of love, I working calmly in love
All summer.

Naming for Love

THESE are the proper names:
Limestone, tufa, coral rag,
Clint, beer stone, braystone,
Porphyry, gneiss, rhyolite,
Ironstone, cairngorm, circle stone,
Blue stone, chalk, box stone,
Sarsen, magnesia, brownstone,
Flint, aventurnine,
Soapstone, alabaster, basalt,
Slate, quartzite, ashlar,
Clunch, cob, gault, grit,
Buhrstone, dolomite,
Flagstone, freestone, sandstone,
Marble, shale, gabbro, clay,
Adamant, gravel, traprock,
And of course brimstone.

Some of the names are shapes:
Crag, scarp, moraine, esker,
Alp, hogback, ledge, tor,
Cliff, boulder, crater,
Gorge, and bedrock.

Some denote uses:
Keystone, capstone,
Hearthstone, whetstone,
And gravestone.

For women a painful stone called
Wombstone, which doctors say is
"A calculus formed in the uterus."
Gallstone and kidneystone hurt everyone.
Millstone is our blessing.

I will not say the names
Of misnamed precious stones.

But a lovely name is gold,
A product of stone.

Underwards is magma;
May all who read this live long.

August 14, 1961

(The day the Brandenburg Gate was shut.)

I PUT my book face down,
And so that I could know
The news while I ate lunch
Turned on the radio.

I heard. I've heard before.
Mike Mansfield asks for calm,
Half muffled in the cries
Clamoring for the bomb.

Sitwell had made the book
To praise the lordly way
Men lived in Angkor Vat.
I'll read no more today.

A Clear Distinction

ONE rash woman who played me false
Apologized, calling herself a bitch,
As if that elegance could expulse
The evil stuck in her heart like pitch.

But style is genius, not aptitude;
Thus Thaïs, bitchery's exquisite,
Portsmouth's duchess with one breast nude,
And Peg the Barmaid, and Antoinette.

These few. The calico rabble stirs,
Flutes chitter in every old sackbut,
And, alas, my lady who so aspires
To become a bitch will remain a slut.

Adolf Eichmann

I WANT no tricks in speaking of this man.
My friends deplore my metaphysical mind,
But now I am a plain and plain-spoken man.

In my life only two men have turned my mind
To vengefulness, and one was this man's chief,
Who was, I now think, probably out of his mind.

But this one is rational. Naturally a mad chief
Needs sane lieutenants. Both were named Adolf,
An ugly Teutonic word which means the chief,

And earlier, in the cold north forest, this Adolf
Meant the wolf, a favorite totem. Let disgrace,
I say, fall for all time to come upon Adolf,

And let no child hereafter bear the disgrace
Of that dirty name. Sometimes in my bed
I study my feet, noticing their disgrace,

For the human foot is an ugly thing. But my bed
Is nothing like the bed that I have seen
Where hundreds of unclothed bodies lay. That bed

Was for dead people, deeply dug, and whoever has seen
Their feet knows the real ugliness and in their voice
Has heard the only true language. I have seen

And I have heard, but my feet live and my voice
Is beautiful and strong, and I say let the dung
Be heaped on that man until it chokes his voice,

Let him be made leprous so that the dung
May snuggle to his bone, let his eyes be shut
With slow blinding, let him be fed his own dung,

But let his ears never, never be shut,
And let young voices read to him, name by name,
From the rolls of all those people whom he has shut

Into the horrible beds, and let his name
Forever and ever be the word for hate,
Eichmann, cast out of the race, a loathsome name

For another kind, a sport spawned in hate
That can never be joined, never, in the world of man.
Lord, forgive me, I cannot keep down my hate.

A Leaf from Mr. Dyer's Woods

I DON'T know why or how
Sometimes in August a maple
Will drop a leaf burned through
Its tender parts with coral
While the veins keep green—
A rare device of color.
When I found such a one
I acted the despoiler,
Taking it from the woods
To give a friend for a trifle,
But her mind was on good deeds
And I turned shy and fearful.

Notes from Robin Hill Cottage

ONE small joy still left
To a writer who has grown wise
In his profession and swift
In the making of similes

Is to discover a word
He has not used before,
An ordinary one just heard
In its whole force and humor.

I think I have not written
The verb *to shed* in all
The twenty years I've given
To saving my wordy soul.

.　　.　　.

As, when I was a drunkard
And staggered to my bed,
Wholly looped and tuckered,
One by one I'd shed

My clothes upon the floor
Until at last, all naked,
I'd tumble with a snore
Into my loyal blankets,

So, when I was reformed
And stumbled onward yet,

Trembling, cold, alarmed,
Then one by one I shed

Each of my heart's desires
Like garments until I fell
Naked among these firs
And the embrace of these hills.

.   .   .

A man is like all earth's fruit,
You preserve him dry or pickled,
It's taking him in and out
That makes him come unbuckled.

.   .   .

Firtrees surround me here,
The deeper woods have ash,
Larch and oak and cedar,
The wild cherry and the beech.

Not mine; no more these walls,
The clapboard or the slate,
That house me on Robin Hill
And another man's estate.

You can't push a metaphor
And I won't speak of clothes,
But my best home so far
Is here in a borrowed house.

.   .   .

Older, yet I am cleanly,
Freer, yet fierce of mind,
And the mountain summer greenly
Calls winter close behind.

.   .   .

I keep a whiskey bottle
Unsealed on my kitchen shelf
For friends who come to tipple
And to tease me and to scoff.

Friends are so often blind,
Or scared to agree in public
That booze and a bullet-wound
Are one to an alcoholic.

We live alone in the cottage,
Married, the bottle and I,
Good mates going down in courage
To die independently.

.   .   .

A bottle's a genial spouse
But in some precise respects
Does not make glad a house;
What manages that is sex.

Now I'm not vain nor choosy,
Miss Marilyn Monroe

[38]

I imagine would be a doozey,
Or La Belle Dame Bardot.

Sometimes such folk are married,
And sometimes not. Me too.
Is your husband shucked—or buried?
Drop by for an interview.

Another Catalogue

ONE OF THE commonest lunacies
That come with age is
Verbomania, and it has many
Forms, including the wild
And horrible verbigeration,
A broken mind repeating
The same words over and over
Like a broken phonograph.
I heard it many times
When I was in the asylum.

I ought to be more careful
About such things, I suppose,
But . . . *fortuna favet fatuis.*

Here is a catalogue
Of products manufactured from
Open hearth and bessemer steel:
Hot rolled billets, blooms,
Slabs, sheet bars, skelp,
Bands, flats, and hexagons,
Rounds, squares, angles, beams,
Tees, zees, and channels,
Agricultural shapes, light weight
Stair stringer channels, and
Many kinds of plates;
Railroad spikes and plates;
Bars for concrete reinforcement;

Forging steel; jalcase steel;
Cold finished rounds, squares,
Hexagons, flats, free cutting
Screw stock, pump rods, and
Shafting (turned and ground,
Turned and polished, or cold
Drawn); junior beams; piling,
Columns, girders, trusses,
Plate work, tanks, barges;
Standard pipe and line pipe,
Casing, tubing, drive and drill
Pipe (lapwelded or seamless);
Wire rods, wire (bright,
Annealed, and galvanized),
Spring wire, barbed wire,
Woven fencing and staples;
And coke tin plate and black
Sheets and other tin mill
And coke by-products.

Inevitable Didactic

THE COTTAGE is small but strongly built,
Slate, brick, and chestnut all the best,
And I curl inside like a child in a quilt,
Cozy and free in my dreams and warm,
As my poems curl, I hope, in their form,
Snugly protected but never oppressed.

R.M.D.

"There's rosemary, that's for remembrance . . ."

SOMEWHERE in the hour
Or two or three
While I was by this flower
Meaning constancy
Seven winds cried in a tower
Hollowly.

This book has been designed and printed by Carroll Coleman at The Prairie Press in Iowa City, Iowa. The body type is hand set Bulmer with Post Titling on the title page. The paper is Ticonderoga laid. This is the twenty-eighth year of book publishing by The Prairie Press.